Original title:
Growth in the Stillness

Copyright © 2025 Creative Arts Management OÜ
All rights reserved.

Author: Lucas Harrington
ISBN HARDBACK: 978-1-80581-830-4
ISBN PAPERBACK: 978-1-80581-357-6
ISBN EBOOK: 978-1-80581-830-4

Contrast in Stillness

In silence, grass tickles the ground,
A snail takes a leap and bounds,
Worms wiggle in a quiet race,
While the trees chuckle at their pace.

The wind tries to gossip with the lake,
But the fish just roll as if awake.
A turtle's thoughts are deeply profound,
While the daisies giggle all around.

Time's Silent Lessons

A clock ticks slow, but hearts race fast,
The tortoise rolls his eyes at the past.
"I'm getting to it," he says with flair,
While the rabbits plot in hasty despair.

Trees whisper secrets in leafy tones,
While squirrels collect their acorn loans.
Lessons learned in a soft, still hum,
As time finds joy in the quiet drum.

Flourishing with the Wind's Breath

The flowers dance like they own the room,
As wind teases them, in a gentle swoon.
Bees buzz around, with gossip to share,
While a daisy pretends she doesn't care.

Grasshoppers leap in a bold ballet,
While lazy clouds drift on their way.
Every sprout with a grip on the ground,
Giggles swell when the sun comes around.

The Quiet Climb

Up the hill, the rocks just sit,
While ants all gather, having a fit.
"Let's form a chain!" one bug did shout,
As they crawl up, there's no doubt.

A snail views each step as a feat,
While a pigeon laughs from the street.
Every inch is a giggly surprise,
In their slow race under bright, amused skies.

Petals of Patience

In a garden where weeds dance,
A snail won a sprint by chance.
Flowers whisper, 'Just take your time,'
While bees buzz by in their own rhyme.

A seed once sulked, 'I'm not a tree!'
But out popped leaves, 'Look at me!'
The sun grinned wide, the rain gave a cheer,
Even the rocks hummed, 'Change is near.'

Birds perched and giggled, 'Is that a bloom?'
'Nah, just a bud playing dress-up in gloom.'
Yet from the dirt, colors took flight,
What a jest, nature's delight!

In slow-motion life, hilarity's found,
The ants held a party on soft ground.
And in the hush, one could see,
That laughter stalks quietly, just like a bee.

The Thrum of Tranquil Time

Tick-tock, what a snooze,
Time's taking its sweet cruise.
A turtle said, 'I'm just fine,'
While a rabbit called him out for a whine.

In the clock's embrace, the minutes conspire,
To laze about near an old campfire.
The shadows chuckle as they stretch and bend,
'We'll take it slow, no need to pretend.'

A sloth slow danced to the rhythm of breeze,
The squirrels looked on, unbothered by tease.
Yet in this slow jam, the world moved as one,
Laughter echoed—oh, what fun!

In the stillness where whispers abound,
Life's secret smiles can always be found.
So stop for a moment, feel the tickle,
And let the wait turn into a giggle.

Roots in the Quiet

Beneath the ground where shadows creep,
Roots tell secrets, oh so deep.
'I'm practically a couch potato!' one claimed,
While another said, 'At least I'm unashamed!'

Tangled together, they share their woes,
'Why'd you grow sideways instead of your toes?'
'At least we're bold,' roots snicker and sway,
'While flowers above, just sway and play!'

The moles laugh loud, digging up dirt,
'Look at those roots, they're comfy in shirt!'
But the roots just chuckle, 'We hold the ground,
While you race about, look at us, we're profound!'

So in the quiet, patience takes hold,
As roots mock the world, so thrilled and bold.
For in the darkness, they're having a ball,
Making the best of it, while standing tall.

Harmonies of the Hidden

In shadows, the music of nature is played,
Where whispers and giggles aren't even delayed.
A raccoon strummed on a tin can lid,
While frogs croaked tunes, all undid the grid.

The crickets chimed in with a click and a clack,
'Let's have a party, no one look back!'
The stars rolled their eyes, 'Oh, what a scene!'
'Can we dance, or are we just mean?'

Every rustle became a new song,
As laughter roamed free, and the night felt long.
Bunnies joined hands, in a two-step glide,
While fireflies twinkled like lights deep inside.

In the hidden corners, mirth filled the air,
As nature's own jesters spread joy everywhere.
So if you listen, you might just find,
The symphony of secrets that spring from the kind.

In the Absence of Sound

In silence, I grew a pet rock,
It stares at me, not a tick or a tock.
We share our thoughts, no need to speak,
It rolls its eyes, I feel so meek.

I tried to teach it how to dance,
But all it did was take a chance.
A wobble here, a shuffle there,
Rock-solid moves, we made quite the pair.

In the stillness, weeds start to smile,
They know they're winning in their own style.
I bring a hoe, they just roll their eyes,
Unfazed by my plans, how time flies!

So here I sit with my stone so cool,
In the absence of sound, I feel like a fool.
But laughter echoes in this quiet retreat,
With a pet that rocks, life is quite sweet.

Layers of Quietude

Underneath the surface, things do crawl,
A snail in a hurry, oh, what a brawl!
It rushed on ahead, then hit a wall,
Turns out it's just taking a call.

Among the leaves, a spider weaves,
Thinking it's a grand architect, but who believes?
Adorned in webs, a shimmery mess,
"I'm not just quiet; I'm a fashion success!"

The flowers chuckle, their petals all prance,
While buzzing bees hold their dance-off glance.
"Who's the best?" the petals tease,
As they sway to the tune of a gentle breeze.

In layers of hush, hilarity reigns,
Nature's antics strike comedy's chains.
With giggles and laughs, life's gig is pure,
In this silent world, fun does endure.

The Imprint of Calm

In tranquil fields where shadows play,
I found a cat who'd lost its way.
"Can't you hear the grass sing?" I asked with glee,
It rolled on its back, said, "Just let me be."

Beneath a tree, an old tortoise sighed,
"Why rush, dear friend? I've got all the time!"
With a slow-motion yawn, it took a bite,
Eating in peace while I chased my plight.

Clouds overhead, they giggle and drift,
Trying to make my worries lift.
"Just float along," they whisper so sweet,
While I wonder if I should put on my cleats.

In stillness, mischief blooms all around,
With laughter and quirks safely tethered and bound.
The imprint of calm has a whimsical touch,
In nature's own jest, we learn not to rush.

Treading Lightly

In the morning dew, I tiptoe around,
A squirrel shrieks, "Hey! That's my mound!"
As I nod and bow, quite the gentle tip,
It mocks my stance with a daring flip.

I tried to sneak past with the grace of a breeze,
But a twig snapped loudly, oh, what a tease!
The world erupted with flutters and barks,
As I giggled and danced, avoiding the sparks.

Even the flowers giggled as I trod,
"Be careful now, tread lightly, you clod!"
They shivered in laughter, but I pressed on,
With the soul of a clown, til the day was gone.

Treading lightly, with humor as my guide,
In this stillness, it's laughter I bide.
Who knew that a stroll could lead to such fun?
In the quiet, we laugh 'til the day is done.

Blossoming Through Stillness

In the garden where time takes a nap,
The daisies giggle at a sleepy gap.
A snail in a tie starts a slow parade,
While the sunbeam's snores make shadows invade.

The roses whisper jokes to the breeze,
While ants form a band, playing tunes with ease.
A cucumber dreams of becoming a star,
Pondering life and just how bizarre!

The leaves are curled up, all snug on a branch,
Telling tales of the squirrels' daring dance.
A frog croaks a laugh, it's a comedic show,
As daisies bob along in a row.

So here in the quiet, joy takes its turn,
In the stillness, the silly ones frolic and learn.

Amidst the Hush

A turtle thinks deep, 'What's the speed of thought?'
While flowers play hide and seek, who would've thought?
A bee steals the scene with its clumsy flight,
And the grass sneezes loud in the warm sunlight.

An acorn dreams big, a tree in its sight,
Counting the years with a giggle of fright.
The worms in the soil throw a dance party,
While a bird's nap above gets quite hearty.

Amidst all the quiet, the laughter rings clear,
As shadows join in with a giggle and cheer.
Each moment a treasure, simple and bright,
In the hush of the garden, pure delight!

Thus the peace around us is more than it seems,
It's a carnival vibe wrapped in stillness and dreams.

Serenity's Subtle Surge

The wind whispers secrets to the trees,
While geese throw a tantrum, on wobbly knees.
A cat takes a pause to consider a nap,
As the clouds up above play a puffy flap.

A flower puts on its most dazzling dress,
Hoping the sun brings forth a sweet caress.
But wait, what's that? A lizard slips by,
With a dance that's more funky than you'd ever try.

Quietly bubbles a brook that can't keep,
A giggle confined, just wanting to leap.
Frogs play the fiddle, all croak and no tune,
While the daisies dance under the bright moon.

So in this calm patch where silliness grows,
Even stillness is a place where laughter flows!

Quietude's Gentle Blossoming

In the still of the morn, when the world isn't loud,
A worm thinks it's winning a race to the cloud.
While daisies debate the best style of sway,
For the title of 'best-dressed' in the yard today.

The sun peeks in, with a wink and a grin,
Inviting the daisies to suddenly spin.
A butterfly flutters, all posh and elite,
Observing a snail scoot its way to a beet.

With whispers of laughter that bloom like the blooms,
The garden erupts in spontaneous flumes.
A soft breeze carries the quirks through the air,
Tickling the petals, with laughter to spare.

In quietude's laughter, so sly and so sweet,
The magic of moments makes life feel complete!

Still Waters

In a pond that's calm and clear,
Fish practice yoga, oh dear!
They stretch their fins with grace and style,
While frogs take selfies, all the while.

A turtle races slowly along,
Singing a tune, all day long.
The water lilies giggle and sway,
As the dragonflies dance in their play.

Secret Lives

In the shadows, crickets rehearse,
A symphony that's somewhat terse.
Worms in tuxedos crawl with flair,
Debating if they should cut the air.

While ants perform a line dance show,
Under moonlight's gentle glow.
Their tiny legs in perfect sync,
Who knew bugs could dance and think?

Buds in the Silence

Buds pop open, quite a tease,
Whispering secrets to the breeze.
Daisies giggle as the tulips pout,
"I swear I heard a bee shout!"

While the sunbeams sip their tea,
The grass sways with glee, carefree.
"Let's throw a party!" the daisies shout,
But the dandelions are all worn out.

The Peaceful Stretch

A snail stretches in a slow, grand way,
"I'm in for the long haul," it seems to say.
Nearby, a cat naps in the sun,
Dreaming of fish, oh what fun!

Clouds drift by in a soft embrace,
While the sun beams down, no need to race.
Time plays tricks, but here we stand,
As the earth spins on, just as planned.

Resilience in the Shadows

Under the stones, moss lives its life,
Avoiding the sunlight's daily strife.
A witty rock shares a pun so bright,
 "Why go out? It's cozy tonight!"

Roots twist and turn, plotting a way,
To sneak a peek at the light of day.
While bunnies bounce to and fro,
In the quiet, a joke steals the show.

The Lull Before the Bloom

In a garden full of snooze,
Flowers slumber, taking cues.
A daisy dreams of afternoon tea,
While the roses plot a jubilee.

The lettuce giggles, taking bets,
On how tall the carrots will get.
Bees snicker as they take their flight,
While worms hold a rave in the moonlight.

The seeds sift through their dreams at night,
Whispering secrets, oh what a sight.
"Who needs sunlight?" a tulip will say,
While pretending to nap the whole day away.

Yet beneath the calm, there's a chat so sly,
Root systems argue, "I'm taller," they lie.
And in this hush, with all this glee,
Life's plotting a story, wait and see!

Soft Measures of Time

Time counts quietly, like a fun game,
Ticks and tocks are all quite the same.
Each second's a joke in a slow-motion film,
While shadows stretch out, tall and slim.

The clouds debate the shape of the day,
One thinks a cat, another a tray.
Grass blades giggle, they're silently rife,
With whispers of wind that tickle to life.

A snail books a trip—oh, what a thrill!
Plans to traverse the garden hill.
While daisies throw a rave by the stone,
Patience, they say, is best done alone.

In this quiet spin, the humor blooms,
With chuckles emerging from leafy rooms.
Time's soft embrace, a carnival dance,
Even a twig gets its chance to prance!

Serene Echoes of Tomorrow

In the stillness of night, secrets curl,
As crickets debate who's the best in the twirl.
The moon winks down at the sleepy grass,
While owls play cards, letting the night pass.

Dreams of the ferns sway, oh what a tease,
"I swear, tomorrow, I'll sprout with ease!"
Laughter tumbles through roots underground,
As the stones gossip, spinning round and round.

Even the stars are in on the fun,
Trading stories when day is done.
Each twinkle a chuckle in the vastness so bright,
Echoes of laughter, a serene delight.

And as dawn creeps in, bright colors unfold,
Nature's humor, a sight to behold.
With every new leaf, a fresh punchline appears,
In the calm of the dawn, it tickles our fears!

A Silent Call to Radiance

In the heart of the quiet, there's a sly little hum,
As flowers plot where the bees will come.
"With nectar for brunch, let's plan a feast,
We'll trickle in sweetness, to say the least!"

Leaves whisper secrets, winding around,
While sunbeams fumble and dance on the ground.
Each petal's a grin, as colors ignite,
In the still where they wait for the morning light.

Sunflowers bob, taking bets on the sun,
"I'll grow taller!" they laugh, "This race will be fun!"
While daisies argue who wore yellow best,
In the calm of the garden, they jest and they jest.

Yet as dawn unfurls, the jokes percolate,
With giggles and chuckles, they cheerfully wait.
In this quiet build-up, there's magic in play,
As nature's own humor makes bright the new day!

Flourishing in the Fade

In the corner of the yard, a weed stands tall,
With dreams of glory, but lacking a ball.
It stretches and bends, and oh what a sight,
Waving to daisies, saying, "I'm alright!"

The flowers roll their eyes, with petals so prim,
While the weed cracks jokes, sounding slightly dim.
"Why chase the sun when it's easier to hide?
Let's make it a party, with no need for pride!"

Butterflies giggle, as the grass starts to sway,
While the weed dances wildly, in a whimsical way.
"Life's not a race, just a chance to be free,
So come join my circus, you know you want to be!"

So in faded glory, the garden's own joke,
Lives a weed with a heart, and laughter it spoke.
For in each little crack, and each tiny crevice,
Whimsy grows wild, in a world that's quite reckless.

Echoes of Unseen Potential

In the shade of a tree, a squirrel has plans,
To build the biggest nest, with just tiny hands.
It hoards up the nuts, swears they're a gold mine,
While birds chuckle softly, "Squirrels are fine!"

With each little leap, it aims for the stars,
Climbing up branches like it's on Mars.
Rags to riches, in a tree made of wood,
Hopes that the acorns will soon turn to food!

The birds take a vote, on who's got the flair,
"A nutty performer! But does it know air?"
With laughter that echoes, around all the trees,
They cheer for the squirrel, with dreams on the breeze.

So potential abounds, in the quiet unseen,
Where silliness thrives, and the grass grows green.
Amidst the wild antics, the joy is sincere,
From a squirrel who dreams, and brings everyone cheer.

Nature's Quiet Ascent

A rock in the garden thinks it's quite wise,
Observing the flowers with unblinking eyes.
It chuckles each day at the bees buzzing round,
"Just wish I had legs, I'd dance on the ground!"

While daisies stretch high to greet morning light,
The rock stays put, and never takes flight.
"It's safer down here, just chill with the ants,
Life's better with snacks, and curious plants!"

The sun offers warmth, as the critters all play,
While the rock sighs heavily, "Do I get a say?"
"Who wants to be fancy with actors so bold?
I'll keep my cool stage, and the stories I've told!"

And though it may grumble, sitting there still,
It knows life is sweet, in a world full of thrill.
For laughter and peace, in each moment we find,
A slow-moving rock can still give joy to the mind!

Seeds of Reflection

In a tiny old pot, a seed starts to plot,
To grow into something! But waits, like a tot.
"Why rush for the sun? Let's lounge and relax,
Dreaming of future — in comfy socks!"

The dirt huffs and puffs, while nearby plants fume,
"Let's stretch our green arms, this isn't a tomb!"
But the seed giggles softly, "Dear friends, just you wait,
I'm building my empire, don't rush to dictate!"

So it rests in the soil, with thoughts oh so grand,
On becoming a tree, with a wide-spreading hand.
In the world of the garden, it let itself be,
As laughter fell gently from bumblebees free.

One day it will rise, with a grin on its face,
But for now it's content, finding joy in the space.
For life can be funny, when you take a short pause,
And plant all the dreams, with a light-hearted cause!

The Softening Earth

In the garden where the weeds play,
Earthworms dance on a sunny day.
Rabbits hold their own parade,
In muddy shoes, they're unafraid.

Old trees gossip, their branches sway,
While bees buzz by in a merry way.
Mushrooms giggle under the dew,
Picking up gossip that's fresh and new.

Nature's choir sings a funny tune,
As squirrels plan for a coconut heist at noon.
With tiny hats and acorn flair,
They steal the show without a care.

So let's embrace the absurdity near,
Where veggies plot plans that are reindeer.
For in the still of a lively earth,
Laughter sprouts alongside rebirth.

Petals Unfurled in Tranquility

Petals stretch like cats in the sun,
Daffodils laugh; it's all in fun.
Tulips argue over best dressed,
While lilacs pretend they're the rest.

In the breeze, a daisy wiggles,
Swaying around, it just giggles.
Butterflies wear their best bow ties,
Stirring up laughter beneath the sky.

Roses blush, all decked in pride,
While daisies hide their roots inside.
A dance of colors, funny and bright,
Together they whisper, 'What a sight!'

In nature's childlike, bright embrace,
Silence crinkles up in laughter's grace.
So let's toast to petals, rooted good cheer,
For in every bloom, humor's near.

Still Waters, Growing Hearts

Ponds reflect puns from above,
As frogs croak jokes, oh how they shove.
Turtles sunbathe with comic flair,
Splashing water, they have no care.

Dragonflies laugh and zip on by,
While fish below start their own sly.
They make bubbles, giggly and light,
A water ballet, quite the sight.

Ripples ripple, mirrors of fun,
Where laughter rises in the sun.
Crickets chirp their comic relief,
As frogs share tales of mischief and grief.

With hearts that expand in serene delight,
Funny antics play over water so bright.
In moments of stillness, they find their part,
Celebrating life in a comedic art.

A Journey Within the Quiet

In the quiet, thoughts begin to dance,
As I trip over chances, lost in a trance.
Whispers of wisdom beneath a tree,
But all I hear is my own sneeze.

Mice share tea in a cozy nook,
Plotting out adventures like a storybook.
With tiny cups, they toast their fears,
As moments stretch into giggling years.

Clouds cuddle up as they float so high,
Playing tag with the birds in the sky.
And as they drift, they whisper and tease,
"Let's land on a cat, just with the breeze."

In the stillness, fun is the cause,
While finding humor in life's little flaws.
So laugh at the quiet, invite it in,
For the journey is funny, let life begin!

Inertia's Unexpected Bloom

In the quiet of my lounging,
A flower grew with no accounting.
It wiggled in the lazy sun,
And said to me, 'Now, isn't this fun?'

I watered it with my cold drink,
While munching on a snack, I think.
The petals laughed, 'This life is grand!'
I raised my glass, we made a stand.

Stagnation? Oh, what a lie,
For things can sprout, if you just try!
A cactus nodded, pride in its spine,
'Who knew that doing nothing's fine?'

So here's a toast to sunny days,
Where blooms arise from lazy ways.
With each slow stretch, I gain a grin,
These roots of joy, they start within.

Echoes of the Undisturbed

In silence, echoes begin to play,
A laugh from a garden tucked away.
'Why rush?' the daisies softly say,
'More time for naps, come what may!'

The earthworms dance, all wiggly glee,
'We're all just chillin', can't you see?'
While bees forget their buzzing spree,
And just hum nice tunes beneath the tree.

A sunflower whispers, 'Take your time!'
As I sip my drink, all feels sublime.
In the stillness, every joke's clear,
Life's funniest punchlines pop right here.

So let the world rush by with haste,
For in this quiet, we make the best taste.
Laughter and blossoms, in gentle tune,
In the calm shadows of the afternoon.

Whispers of Quiet Dawn

The morning yawns, a sleepy sight,
Dew drops giggle, feeling just right.
The sun stretches, a lazy cat,
It tickles the flowers, 'Imagine that!'

A snail speeds slow—well, maybe not,
While grass blades dance, in a tender plot.
They tickle toes of wandering ants,
Whispering dreams of wildflower chants.

With every breeze, a chuckle's found,
In this still air where giggles abound.
A squirrel chimes in, with thistly cheer,
'Why hurry, friends? We have all year!'

So here we stand, in pauses sweet,
Finding joy in every heartbeat.
In the quiet dawn, with laughter sprawled,
Life blooms brighter, not at all stalled.

Budding in Solitude

In the comfort of my cozy chair,
A plant peeked up with leafy flair.
'Stop scrolling, it's time to unwind!'
I chuckled, thinking it's one of a kind.

It waved its leaves like a fan at a show,
While I pretended like I didn't know.
The flowers snickered, 'We're here for a laugh!'
In my stillness, they found their path.

A rock said, 'I'm holding my place!'
While dirt chimed in, 'It's a slow-paced race!'
The worms just winked, as they dug around,
In solitude, joy is truly found.

So let's raise a pot, to the lazy crew,
For every moment spent, brings something new.
In the hush, we thrive just like the bloom,
In our silly world, there's always room.

In the Calm of Night

Under the moon's gaze, we silently creep,
Dreaming of castles, or maybe a sheep.
The stars trace our laughter, like lines on a map,
While squirrels in pajamas take turns on a nap.

The shadows play tricks, they dance and they weave,
A cat with a monocle seems to believe.
He chuckles at mice that tiptoe around,
A moonlit parade where madness is found.

In soft whispers of grass, the crickets conspire,
To sing silly songs, elevating the choir.
Each giggle a note, in the evening so bright,
Creating a symphony through pure delight.

So here in the calm, under starlit delight,
We find joy in the whispers of the quiet night.
For even in stillness, there's humor to find,
In the dance of the dusk, where laughter's unconfined.

Softly, the World Awakens

As dawn tiptoes in with a wink and a grin,
The coffee pot bubbles, let chaos begin!
A rooster is strutting in socks and a hat,
Declaring the morning, absurd as a cat.

The flowers unfold, they stretch and they yawn,
With petals like pajamas, they greet the dawn.
A bee in a bowtie buzzes with flair,
As butterflies giggle, floating through the air.

Trees whisper secrets, their leaves in a spin,
While squirrels with acorns are plotting to win.
The sun gives a chuckle, painting skies bright,
In this playful circus, everything feels right.

So softly the world stirs, in this fun little play,
Where laughter and joy welcome each new day.
In the rhythm of morning, there's mischief galore,
As the universe wakes, we keep wanting more.

The Bloom of Inner Time

Deep in the soil, where silliness sprouts,
A snail in sunglasses lounges about.
He tells jokes to the daisies, who giggle with glee,
As ants do a dance, oh what a sight to see!

Time trickles slowly, like syrup on toast,
The flowers roll over, let's celebrate most!
A dandelion's wish whispers softly, 'Be bold!'
While butterflies chuckle, their stories retold.

In this garden of dreams, where laughter is prime,
A worm tells a tale of his youth—oh, so sublime!
With each little bloom, there's a giggle or two,
A riot of colors, all born from the dew.

So cherish the moments where silliness climbs,
In the bloom of our hearts, we create silly rhymes.
Let time be a jester, a friend in disguise,
Whispering whimsies beneath sunny skies.

Serenity's Embrace

In quiet corners, the slippers do dance,
A hedgehog named Kevin is lost in a trance.
He's dreaming of pies that float through the air,
With whipped cream clouds and laughter to share.

Resting on cushions stuffed full of delight,
Where all of our worries take wing and take flight.
Chickens in tutus strut round in a line,
Quacking out ballads, oh isn't it divine?

The rhythm of peace is a waltz in disguise,
With bubbles of joy that tickle the skies.
As sunbeams throw parties with guests made of light,
We twirl in the stillness, hearts giddy and bright.

So embrace this charm, where humor runs free,
In serenity's arms, we find our own glee.
For laughter the best, in soft, tender space,
Will forever remind us of joy's sweet embrace.

Unraveling in Silence

In a garden where squirrels play,
The flowers giggle, night and day.
A snail slides by with a big old grin,
Saying, 'Look at me, I've found my kin!'

Rabbits whisper secrets low,
While unbothered bees hum to and fro.
The shadows dance, so sly and spry,
Wishing they could join the sky.

Underneath the leafy swirl,
A clump of dirt begins to twirl.
Worms throw parties with glee and zest,
Claiming stillness is truly the best!

There's humor found in quiet things,
Like ants who wear imaginary wings.
In this calm, the laughter swells,
As nature spins its soft, sly spells.

The Peace of Becoming

On a calm day, the pond just giggles,
With frogs who leap and do their wiggles.
The dragonflies wear hats of style,
And hover around like they own the aisle.

Leaves whisper tales of the great unknown,
While turtles plot how to rule their throne.
As grass blades stretch, they tickle the breeze,
"Getting taller's not hard, just eat your peas!"

Sunshine winks, a playful tease,
Upon dandelions doing as they please.
They puff their cheeks and blow out dreams,
While worms rehearse for their night-time gleams.

In this quiet place, the laughter flows,
With every root and every rose.
The world may hush, but inside it roars,
In the stillness, mischief adores.

Hidden Currents

Beneath the still, a tickle stirs,
As fish play tag without a blur.
The turtles jest, spinning rounds,
Declaring victory in puddle bounds.

Mice in shadows keep their score,
Cracking jokes that leave you wanting more.
They gather 'round for a giggling spree,
"Who knew peace could sound like a snore?"

A breeze swoops in with a cheeky grin,
While flowers gently dance with a spin.
"Hey, watch out—here comes a bee!"
"Oh please, just let me be free!"

From every nook, the echoes twine,
In a silent party, all divine.
Where nature hums and laughter pulses,
In hidden currents, joy repulses.

The Growth of Quiet Dreams

In a meadow soft, where daisies sip,
A breeze stirs tales with each tiny twip.
Beetles boast of plans they hatch,
While sun in splendor helps them match.

Clouds sport hats, quite funky and wide,
As they float, they giggle with pride.
"Is it sunny? Or shall we rain?"
"Oh come now, stop—it's all just for gain!"

The roots below do a limber dance,
Chasing dreams in the earth's expanse.
"Let's grow tall, but keep it low-key,
In the quiet, we're wild, you see?"

Stars peek through with a wink and cheek,
Whispering secrets they dare not speak.
In stillness wrapped, the laughter beams,
For hidden life is sewn in dreams.

Transitions in Twilight

In shadows, ants hold a conference,
With tiny ties and a grand pretense.
Discussing crumbs and evening plans,
Oh, the joy of tiny clans.

Breezes tease the dandelions,
Fluffing up their fine fine lines.
They dance around with such delight,
Falling over, oh what a sight!

A flower sleeps beneath the trees,
Snoring softly in the breeze.
Dreaming not of blooming soon,
But of late-night chats with the moon.

In twilight's grip, the world unwinds,
With playful friends in funny minds.
Even the stars break into grins,
For night can hide the silliest sins.

The Growth of Gentle Dreams

In the garden, a snail makes a speech,
About life's lessons, no need to breach.
He says, 'Take it slow, you'll get there too,'
While munching leaves, as snails often do.

A sleepy cat with a heart so grand,
Dreams of being a rock band.
With a purring beat and a scratchy string,
His concerts are a funny thing!

Beneath the shade, the daisies plot,
To rise and shine, oh, they are hot!
But they giggle while sunbathing wide,
Knowing the fun of a lazy ride.

So take a tip from this silly tale,
In the stillness, the dreams set sail.
Your funny thoughts are meant to sprout,
Just like the leaves when the sun's about.

Inactive Currents

A stream of thoughts without a rush,
Just floating by in a gentle hush.
The fish exchange their witty banter,
'Hey, what's with this lack of canter?'

Clouds lounge like kings above the hill,
Sipping sunshine, oh what a thrill.
They take their time, they hardly move,
Making lazy rhythms that groove.

The lily pads hold a poker game,
Where frogs bet bug bites with no shame.
They laugh and leap at the silly stakes,
With dreams of flies for their belly aches.

In the stillness, life slows down,
We find the funny in a worn-out frown.
For even when things seem to pause,
Laughter helps to hide the flaws.

The Subtle Push

A tiny seed breaks through the frost,
With a wink, it claims, 'I'm never lost!'
It stretches out with leafy glee,
Saying, 'Look at me! I'm wild and free!'

Bumblebees take their midday break,
Sipping nectar with a little shake.
They share tales of floral perks,
While plotting out some cheeky works.

A mole beneath, with grand designs,
Constructs a maze with twisty lines.
'More tunnels, more snacks,' he chuckles bold,
In the dark, adventures unfold.

In subtle pushes, laughter sneaks,
We find joy in the stillness speaks.
Nature whispers jokes, so fine,
After all, the punchline's divine!

Unfolding in Silence

In a garden where whispers play,
The daisies giggle, come what may.
A snail takes its time, oh so slow,
While the grass keeps telling jokes below.

The sun pokes fun at clouds so shy,
Like a child who holds a secret high.
Each leaf has its tale, every twig its song,
In this silent dance where we all belong.

The breeze makes the branches sway just right,
As squirrels start planning their weekend flight.
With a chuckle, the flowers bloom anew,
Their petals giggle in a vibrant hue.

Amongst giggles and nature's cheer,
Even the crickets laugh—can you hear?
Life's a circus in quiet delight,
Underneath the stars, bright, blithe, and light.

Waiting for the World

Time ticks softly, a clock on the wall,
A turtle ponders, should it crawl?
The daisies debate who's more sprightly,
While the chipmunks snack rather lightly.

A cat naps on the sunlit mat,
Dreaming of fish—imagine that!
While ants in a line, on a crumb they feast,
Each of them hoping for a cake at least.

Clouds drift by, wearing comical hats,
Conspiring with pigeons and lazy cats.
A butterfly winks at the sleeping bees,
As they all share secrets beneath the trees.

Waiting for the world to wake and play,
With a dash of silly, come what may.
In this funny realm where time is slow,
Every moment's a show, don't you know?

Forms of the Quiet Mind

Beneath the surface, ideas grow,
Like silly balloons all in a row.
Thoughts tumble around, frolicking free,
Creating new shapes, come check and see.

The clouds sketch stories on the blue,
Of knights and dragons, oh what a view!
They reshape themselves just for a laugh,
Like kids playing games in a quiet gaff.

In shadows and shades, they quietly spin,
Imaginations dance where we begin.
Turn thoughts 'round until they're quite dizzy,
And watch as the world gets a bit busy.

In the stillness, where no one peeks,
The secrets of laughter play hide and seek.
So ponder away in your peace of mind,
And see where the silly leads you to find.

Growth in the Gaps

In the cracks of the pavement, plants sprout fast,
With a wink and a grin, they'll outlast.
Between the sighs and the silent breaks,
Life sings its tune, oh what it takes!

A cozy weed winks at the concrete shy,
"Don't you wish you could be spry?"
While dandelions throw a party each day,
Inviting the sun to come out and play.

With laughter held tight in the space between,
The roots dig down deep; they're quite the scene.
In every little crevice, joy can sneak,
Creating a world where life feels unique.

So hunt for the gaps, let your smiles flow,
In every small corner, let kindness grow.
With a chuckle and a cheer, just take a leap,
In the laughter of life, there's magic to keep.

Buds in the Calm

In the quiet, buds do peek,
Not a sound, but a cheeky tweak.
With a giggle, they stretch and yawn,
Waking softly, break of dawn.

No one's rushing, no one's loud,
Our buddy buds have formed a crowd.
They dance in silence, sly and spry,
Looking for a reason why.

Down with the worms, they start to chat,
"Can you believe we're chatting like that?"
They jibe, they jab, in very low tones,
While watching the fluff of fluffy drones.

The calmness blankets them all around,
In this hush, joy can be found.
So let's giggle in this chill,
For in the stillness, we find our thrill!

Flourish in Solitude

A leaf all alone in a cozy nook,
Reads a book like a fancy crook.
Sipping dew from a tiny mug,
As ants march on with a playful shrug.

Suddenly, a breeze gives a cheer,
"Hey leaf, no need for any fear!"
And off it twirls with a dizzy dance,
Spinning round like it's in a trance.

The shadows giggle from nearby trees,
"Look at the leaf, it's got such ease!"
No pressure here to bloom or flee,
Just sipping sun, feeling so free.

So let the world spin and swirl,
The leaf just laughs, gives a twirl.
In this quiet, fun can be found,
Where whimsy flourishes all around!

Roots of Reflection

Buried deep where it's cozy,
Roots gather round, feeling nosy.
"What's the fuss up there in the sun?"
"I hear giggles and thoughts on the run!"

With every wiggle, they share a jest,
"Who knew the ground would be such a fest?"
They tickle each other, whispering right,
While leaves party on, much to their delight.

Up on the surface, flowers sway,
While roots giggle, anyway.
"No need for sunlight," one does quip,
"In this rich soil, we've got the grip!"

So let the laughter seep through the ground,
Among the roots, joy is unbound.
In quiet corners, they're never alone,
For in reflection, humor has grown!

Gentle Ascent

Little sprouts climb with a grin,
Taking their time as the fun begins.
"Hey, look, Ma! I'm reaching the sky!"
"Hold still, you silly! Do you want to fly?"

Each tiny bud with dreams in their head,
Chasing clouds, where laughter is spread.
Swirling to heights where giggles bounce,
Playing hide and seek with the clouds' pounce.

"How high can we go?" they shout with glee,
While birds pass by, hooting, "Let us see!"
But sprouts just chuckle, as they ascend,
For every climb brings laughter to bend.

So up they rise, in a gentle spin,
Finding joy in every little win.
In the stillness, hearts feel light,
For in their world, everything's bright!

Solitary Blossoms

In a garden all alone, a flower did bloom,
It wore a bright hat and sang in the gloom.
A bee came to dance, quite tipsy, it seems,
But tripped on a petal, and fell—what a dream!

A snail with a smile watched the whole scene play,
Sipping on dew like it's fine cabaret.
With laughter the breeze tickled petals in cheer,
While ants in tuxedos lined up for a beer!

The sun peeked and giggled from clouds full of fluff,
Said, "You've got to admit, this life can be tough!"
But each little bloom joined the merriment spree,
Their roots bustled softly, like friends at a tea.

Thus blooms in their quiet found joy in the jest,
While soil held the secrets, so snug and so pressed.
A garden of laughter, they danced to their tune,
In the stillness, they thrived, as silly as noon.

The Unseen Rise

Under layers of earth, a seed said, "Just wait!"
To a worm strumming dirt like it's some kind of fate.
"I'll pop up like toast, just you wait and see,"
Said the sprout trying hard, feeling quite carefree.

While the roots engaged in a ticklish race,
A rock claimed the throne—"I've got the best place!"
But the seed rolled its eyes, quite ready to play,
"You'll be rocked by my bloom; it'll be quite a day!"

The sun peeked in laughter, casting smiles all around,
Said, "Let's make this a dance, springing up from the ground!"
So each playful sprout, though unseen and so shy,
Laughed at the notion of waving goodbye.

Eager leaves emerged with a wink and a twirl,
Stirring clouds of confusion in this bright spring whirl.
As jokes bloomed in silence, they sparkled — how sweet!

In the stillness, they rose, on their tiny green feet.

Serenity's Secret Garden

In a patch of pure quiet, a dandelion pried,
Its fluffy white head said, "Come on, take a ride!"
The breeze giggled back, "You're silly, you know,
But let's see how far we can play like a show!"

While daisies compared hats, their petals all bright,
A ladybug laughed, turned the day into night.
"You think you are fancy?" a tulip did scoff,
"But I can do jazz hands! Just watch, get your scoff!"

Sunshine sprinkled laughter all over their faces,
As shadows danced lightly, revealing their graces.
Each plant shared a secret, each rooted in jest,
Whispering jokes in their magical quest.

In this secret retreat where the laughter run wild,
Serenity bloomed; each leaf felt like a child.
With petals of joy and roots in the fun,
They thrived in their stillness, united as one.

Beneath the Surface

Beneath a thick layer, the roots had a ball,
Conferencing whispers on how to stand tall.
One declared boldly, "I'm going for gold!"
While another just giggled, "Just do as you're told!"

A squirrel passed by, munching acorns with glee,
He heard all their plotting and said, "Let it be!"
But the roots felt so clever, with plans all so grand,
They schemed and they laughed, with dirt on their hands.

When raindrops came tumbling, they gushed with delight,

"We've cracked the top code—let's party tonight!"
But mud meant no moonlight and twisted their dance,
Yet somehow, they thrived, adding giggles to chance.

So when spring finally came and pulled back the door,
Out burst the green laughter; they couldn't ignore.
In the hush of the earth, they sparked a merry spree,
For joy can be found wherever you see.

Echoing Potential

In a small corner, a seed had a dream,
It giggled and wiggled, oh what a meme!
It whispered to raindrops, 'Come dance with me!'
And that tiny sprout thought, 'I'm as big as a tree!'

A snail rolled by, laughing so bright,
'You're just getting started, have you seen the height?'
The sprout just chuckled, all green and spry,
'Wait till I grow, I'll be reaching the sky!'

Sunbeams tickled its leaves, all in a race,
While clouds played peek-a-boo, giving sad frowns a chase.
And as days turned to weeks, the laughter rang clear,
'Conclusion: I'll outgrow all the silly old deer!'

As the blooms made a party, the garden turned wild,
The sprout winked at the moon: 'Look, this isn't so mild!'
With petals like party hats, so vibrant and bright,
A testament of joy in the soft, gentle night.

The Whispering Path

On a path less traveled, a pebble stood still,
Dreaming of adventures, with quite a strong will.
'You'll see me one day!' it sang with delight,
As ants turned to giants in the soft morning light.

The grass grew tall, thinking it was the best,
Proclaiming, 'Grow, dear pebble, you'll outshine the rest!'

But ole' pebble chuckled, 'I've got my own plan,
When I roll down a hill, I'll be faster than man!'

The breeze chimed in with a tickle and tease,
'This path is your stage, just do what you please.'
And as clouds floated by, they chuckled and sighed,
Isn't growth in the stillness quite a fun ride?

So the pebble gathered courage, a little quite bold,
Dreaming of the places and stories untold.
'Just you wait!' it yelled, as it leaned all the way,
'I'll throw a rock concert and dance on display!'

Nestled in the Quiet

In a pocket of silence, a turtle took rest,
Wearing a cap made of leaves, it felt like a jest.
With moss on its shell, it claimed it was chic,
'The trendiest creature! I'm quite unique!'

The flowers around, they chimed in delight,
'Slow down, little buddy, don't start a fight!'
With a wink and a grin, and a little shake,
The turtle retorted, 'I'm here for the break!'

As whispers of nature played soft lullabies,
The critters all gathered, wide-opened eyes.
They laughed 'til they cried, at a turtle so sly,
Nestled in quiet, reaching for the sky.

So remember, dear friends, when life feels too loud,
A little retreat can make you feel proud.
For even in stillness, hilarity thrives,
In quietude's garden, our silliness thrives!

Growth Amidst the Fading Light

In the garden, weeds have found their place,
They dance with joy, a clumsy embrace.
Sunset chuckles, the shadows look spry,
As daisies giggle and fireflies fly.

The turtle crawls with a swagger so bold,
While rabbits debate if the night's getting cold.
Crickets compose a symphony grand,
Each note a quirk from the nighttime band.

They've mastered the art of the leisurely crawl,
In this twilight hour, they've made a big call.
Why rush and fuss when there's fun to be had?
In every slow step, the world's just a tad mad!

So here's to the night, with its silly old charms,
Life may be fleeting, but it dances in arms.
In fading light, there's laughter around,
As plants and their pals get lost and are found.

Breathing in the Quiet

In a breeze that whispers secrets untold,
A snail sips tea while the sun's growing bold.
The leaves are debating what shade they should wear,
While woodpeckers tap like they just don't care!

A cat in a sunbeam thinks deeply, or not,
She's plotting ways to surprise her pet slot.
With each mindful pause, there's a chuckle so sweet,
As time takes a breather on soft little feet.

The river hums softly, a tune just for frogs,
While turtles play poker and hang out with logs.
Nature's chic party, no need for a rush,
In this hushed celebration, all join in the hush.

So when life tries to hustle, remember the game,
There's joy in the quiet, a peaceful acclaim.
With laughter and stillness, they're all intertwined,
As nature jiggles, so wonderfully maligned.

In the Pause, a Promise

A squirrel downtown slows for a snack,
Pausing to ponder, foot on the track.
He wonders if nuts are the best thing to steal,
As the robins chirp, 'What's the next meal deal?'

Time takes a timeout, whispers so low,
While ants hold a meeting, they're planning a show.
They stamp their tiny feet, plotting surprise,
As flowers shake their heads, 'Oh, those little guys!'

A butterfly winks at the clouds up above,
While rain starts to giggle, feeling quite love.
They share a soft moment, a pause in their flight,
In the midst of the chaos, they find pure delight.

With every slow breath, it's a quirky ballet,
As nature invites us to join in the play.
In a moment so still, laughter could bloom,
For life's just a jest in this wide, wacky room.

The Heart of Silence

In the hush of a dawn, the frogs start their chat,
As a wise old owl hoots, 'What's up with that?'
The daisies stretch yawning, 'Oh, another day!'
While a slug simply shrugs and slides off to play.

The clouds look unsure, should they rumble or rain?
While a beetle files taxes, they're all feeling plain.
A lone cricket laughs, 'We'll make it a show!'
As time ticks along, moving briskly and slow.

The stillness erupts in a joyous ballet,
With branches that jive and flowers at play.
Each giggle and wiggle is a wink from the earth,
In the heart of this silence, we discover their mirth.

So give a good chuckle when life feels too tight,
Remember the gardens all dance in the light.
Amidst all the calmness, a ruckus can bloom,
In this beautiful silence, it's the brightest room.

The Art of Pausing

In the garden where I sit,
Weeds dance wildly, what a fit!
Lazily they sway and play,
While I munch on chips all day.

The bulb I planted last July,
Thinks it's time to say goodbye.
Yet here I wait, all snug and warm,
While roots plot their next big charm.

The sun won't rush, it takes its time,
A sloth competing in a climb.
But in this lull, I sip my tea,
And giggle at the lazy spree.

Here's to patience, my dear friend,
In doing nothing, we transcend.
As flowers bloom and leaves take bows,
I'll recline here, let's make vows.

Silent Awakening

The trees are yawning, just like me,
In morning light, they stretch with glee.
A squirrel naps on branch so high,
While dreaming dreams that touch the sky.

I sip my coffee, slow and thick,
As petals wink, a subtle trick.
They tease the bee who's out too soon,
In search of nectar, clutching tunes.

The pond reflects a sleepy frog,
Who croaks a beat; oh, what a slog!
But here we sit, the world's on pause,
In this bizarre and quiet cause.

Nature's clock ticks soft and slow,
As lazy breezes come and go.
In silence, things begin to sing,
Life's a laugh, a gentle fling.

Nature's Hidden Pulse

The flowers plot a sneak attack,
While I just lounge, thinking, 'What's the hack?'
They pop their heads, with colors bright,
Each petal laughing at my plight.

The tree stands tall with sturdy grace,
While roots below write, 'Slow down, ace.'
A hedgehog rolls, he's lost the plot,
Snoozing away, he cares not a jot.

Birds chirp jokes, I swear it's true,
About the worm that ate his shoe.
Yet here I sit, with snacks and shade,
While all around, the jokes are made.

Nature's rhythm makes me grin,
As I find joy in not being in.
With laughter, it curates the day,
So let it be, come what may.

Resilience in Repose

The cactus donned a sleepy hat,
While pondering where the sun went at.
His prickly friends are snug and tight,
Snoring soft 'neath the moonlight's bite.

A snail slides by, with gusto rare,
He whispers soft, 'I have no care.'
Each step a joke, a waddle spree,
While daisies snicker, 'Look at he!'

The bumblebee buzzes in his dream,
He's late for work, but what a scheme!
In pause, he finds the sweetest grace,
And laughs aloud at the frantic race.

So here's to rest, a funny spice,
In nature's arms, all feels so nice.
From petals to the moonlit glee,
I'll nap and laugh—just let me be!

Whispers of Quietude

In the garden where nobody treads,
A flower snickers, pretending to spread.
"Why so still?" a bee drones along,
"Just waiting for silence to hum me a song."

With giggles, the roots shake in their bed,
Plotting their antics, all green and red.
"Why rush to bloom?" the petals begin,
"Let's savor the dirt and the laughs from within."

Blossoms Beneath the Silence

In a pot with no sunshine around,
A cactus named Chuck made comedy sound.
"I'm not just prickles!" he proudly did state,
"With patience like this, I'll soon be first-rate!"

Oh, the peonies plotted in whispers so sly,
"Let's stir up a ruckus or give it a try!"
While daisies giggled and twirled in a trance,
Waiting for moments when stillness could dance.

The Unseen Rise

Deep underground where the daylight won't peek,
A sprout named Tim had a sense of the cheek.
"Why reach for the sun?" he shouted with glee,
"I'll find my own way, just you wait and see!"

The snails laughed as they slid past his fate,
"Oh Tim, just lie low, it's the way to be great!"
In the quiet, he flexed, not a moment too late,
A little green miracle just couldn't wait.

Echoes of Serenity

In the calm where the elk softly prance,
The wildflowers gathered for a wild dance.
"Who needs loud music?" a daisy declared,
"We'll groove with the breezes, and we won't be snared!"

The grasses were rustling, a symphony grand,
With laughter that rippled across the whole land.
"Stay quiet and joyful, it's what we adore,
In the hush of the woods, we're never a bore!"

The Silent Bloom

In a garden where whispers play,
A flower sneezes in its own way.
It hops up and down, a quirky spree,
Saying, "Look at me, I'm fresh and free!"

The ants chuckle as they dance around,
A patch of dirt is the best playground.
With petals bright, they mock the sun,
"Why so serious? Let's have some fun!"

The raindrops tap like a cheeky drum,
While little worms wiggle, feeling numb.
"We're all here to bask in the glow,"
Said the sleepy bee with a joyful flow.

And in this strange, delightful scene,
The silent bloom knows where it's been.
With laughter thick in the air so warm,
Nature's humor is its own charm.

Embracing the Echoes

In shadows where echoes always hum,
A snail shouts proudly, "I'm not so dumb!"
It slides through mud with a goofy grace,
"I'm racing the beetles, let's pick up the pace!"

The grass stands tall, but wobbly still,
"Watch me bend like I'm a thrill-seeking hill!"
With every breeze, it giggles aloud,
"I'm more than a lawn, I'm a grassy crowd!"

Birds share jokes with the breezy air,
"Why did the leaf go to town without a pair?"
It danced on branches, all twist and twine,
"Because I had roots and preferred to dine!"

In echoes, they find the sound of their cheer,
Each note a reminder that joy is near.
So let's laugh together, no frowns, just fun,
In the symphony played by each ray of sun.

Awakening beneath the Calm

The morning stretches with a sleepy yawn,
A muffins' aroma dances on the lawn.
The toast laughs loudly as it pops up high,
Saying, "I'm the breakfast that'll surely fly!"

A curious bug climbs up a long leaf,
"What's this life? Is it joy or grief?"
But the leaf replies with a whimsical sway,
"It's a ride, my friend, come join the play!"

All the petals nod in a sleepy hue,
"Let's throw a party; we're fun-loving too!"
With every rustle, they chuckle along,
Creating a symphony, a merry song.

And as the sun blankets all with its light,
Nature laughs on through the day and night.
Thus waking beneath this carefree charm,
Find laughter and joy, free from alarm.

Flourish in the Hushed Hours

Under the twilight, where shadows prance,
A gopher in pajamas begins to dance.
It twirls around, with a chuckle and grin,
Saying, "Who knew where the fun would begin?"

The moon snickers, a playful old friend,
"Shhhh! We're quiet, but don't need to bend!"
The stars join in, each twinkle so bright,
"In hushed hours, there's laughter in sight!"

Ferns wiggle their fronds in a secret show,
"We're not shy, we're just taking it slow!"
In the hush, they find their own lively way,
Creating a riot in a tranquil sway.

So gather round, in the still of the night,
Where even the silence has a delight.
For in these hours, where whispers are found,
Laughter blooms softly, a joyous sound.

Echoes of Forgotten Seasons

In winter's grip, we sip our tea,
A leaf insists it still can flee.
Snowflakes giggle, soft and bright,
Their dance delays the morning light.

The daffodils have lost their way,
Suggesting sun on a cloudy day.
A squirrel's grin, a cheeky stare,
While they plot mischief in the air.

Old pumpkins laugh at squirrels' pranks,
Instead of fright, they form new ranks.
By spring they'll wear a crown of green,
With cheeky jests that can't be seen.

So here we stand, in leafy hood,
With jokes that sprout from hillside wood.
The seasons speak in hushed delight,
While we await the next big night.

The Palette of Silence

There's humor found in quiet hues,
Where giggling grass finds clever clues.
Unmoved by noise, it speaks in grin,
Each color whispers where to begin.

The bluebird chuckles from a tree,
Sketching laughter on the breeze, you see.
While daisies hold a secret sway,
In softest tones, they play all day.

The sunset drapes a laughing cloak,
With orange giggles—oh, what a joke!
Each flicker hints at tales unspun,
A canvas waiting, just for fun.

In muted shades, the world rejoices,
While flowers huddle, share their voices.
So take a moment, pause to thrive,
Where silence paint's that sneaky vibe.

When Waiting Breathes

A tortoise wears a crown of dreams,
While ants plot routes with giggling schemes.
In stillness lies a vibrant jest,
Where slowing down is truly best.

The clock winks with a playful sigh,
As minutes dance and quickly fly.
Patience chuckles, grows a grin,
For while we wait, life's fun begins.

A tree pauses, stretches wide,
Its leaves are playing hide and slide.
Waiting may seem a heavy chore,
But it's where laughter lifts and soars.

So when you find yourself held tight,
Remember this: stillness feels just right.
Embrace the plot twists life may weave,
And find the joy that we can cleave.

The Journey within Stillness

In the quiet corners of a room,
A sock debates its fate and doom.
While dust bunnies plot a daring flight,
They spin their tales of pure delight.

Amidst the stillness, ideas sprout,
Like flamingos practicing a shout.
The couch becomes a ship, they say,
Sailing through dreams in wobbly play.

Thoughts bubble up like a hot stew,
Stirred by whispers of what to do.
In the pause, absurdity's born,
As the world outside begins to mourn.

So take the time, let laughter swell,
In moments of silence, magic will dwell.
As you wander through the day's mild thrill,
A journey awaits, so take a chill.

Embracing the Void

In the garden of my mind, I sow,
Tiny ideas that giggle and grow.
They sprout in silence, not making noise,
Tickling the edges of my thoughts like toys.

In the quiet, they play hide and seek,
Nudging my soul, making me sneak.
With each little spark, I start to grin,
Who knew the void could be such a win?

A whisper of laughter fills the air,
As dreams don puzzles with crazy flair.
I twirl in circles, not a care in sight,
In the hush of the void, I feel so light.

So here's to the silence, the calm that it brings,
Where even the nothing has its own swings.
In the deep of the quiet, I dance and rejoice,
In the void, I'm found—oh, what a choice!

The Unfurling Mystery

Once a seed hid in the earth like a spy,
Sneaking dreams under the vast, blue sky.
In shadows of doubt, it quietly sat,
Pondering if it should grow into a cat.

With the tickle of sun and a patter of rain,
The seed giggled softly, feeling the gain.
Unfurling its humor, it reached for the light,
With leafy applause, it danced into sight.

A comical twist, a potato in bloom,
Twirled with daisies, the garden's wild room.
And though it was messy, it made quite a scene,
Who knew dirt could sprout something so green?

In the theater of nature, laughter takes flight,
As whispers of wonder bop left and right.
In the unfurling, secrets play tag,
Mystery's funny, with a colorful rag!

A Lullaby for New Beginnings

Hush now, dear dreams, take a snooze,
In the cozy cocoon where the old one brews.
Sleep soundly, while ribbons of hope,
Wrap tightly around you, like a slippery rope.

Tossed by the winds, you'll twist and glide,
Finding your rhythm in the merry tide.
As crickets serenade you with their tunes,
You'll wake with a chuckle, dancing with moons.

Oh, the new is a jester in a colorful hat,
Waking with giggles, imagine that!
While stars wink and whisper the softest tales,
New beginnings wear shoes with sparkly trails.

So rest, little dreams, let the night be your guide,
Tomorrow you'll frolic, with joy far and wide.
In the sweet lull of slumber, have the best of times,
Awakening next to silly nursery rhymes!

The Dance of Timelessness

In a realm where clocks spin upside down,
The hours wear pajamas and turtleneck gowns.
They dance like children at the edge of a dream,
With giggles of time in an odd little theme.

Old moments and new, they shimmied about,
Swapping their secrets, forgetting their doubt.
Each tick-tock twirled, in an absurd way,
A conga line made of yesterday's play.

While stillness cackled like a wise old fox,
The future skipped rope with a playful paradox.
Together they swayed, like grass in a breeze,
In the dance of the ages, we laugh with ease.

So if you find yourself caught in a spin,
Join in the laughter, let the fun begin!
In whimsical cycles, we find our place,
In timeless pirouettes, we all find our grace.

www.ingramcontent.com/pod-product-compliance
Lightning Source LLC
Chambersburg PA
CBHW070316120526
44590CB00017B/2708